I0170881

Many, many people have a hand in every Great Fire. Associates, co-workers, friends, and family— my four boys and my beautiful, loving wife of twenty-seven years—all made this book possible.

But it is to my parents that I dedicate this book. Mr. Otis Carver Dickinson and Mrs. Dealma Watts Dickinson, I dedicate this, my first book, to you, because you both have made me who I am. Your dedication to life, love, and happiness moves me to tears. You are the best examples of family that I can pattern after.

Contents

A Hero Named Bill Pickett

Bill Pickett was a real American hero. His life story shows how normal people can become real heroes from just doing the right thing. And it reminds us that some heroes become well known, some remain unknown, but every person is created to do something heroic.

Like Bill Pickett, you and I must strive to reach our full potential and become heroes. This book reveals many key elements to having and living a full and successful life. So listen closely.

Bill Pickett is famous for being the first

bulldogger. He invented the rodeo technique of throwing a cow to the ground by twisting its head and biting its lip. Pickett became famous all around the world for bulldogging. A movie was made about him in the 1920s (*The Bull-Dogger*), and in 1994 the United States Postal Service put his picture on a stamp series (Legends of the West).

To the best of my research, everything in this story is true, even though many might call some parts *hyperbole*. (Look it up!) I've read many books and news articles; I've viewed many video summaries; I've spoken to a few surviving family members; I've interviewed a few people who have seen Bill Pickett perform; and I've told this story over 300 times to well over 20,000 people! It is one of my favorite stories to tell in my family's unique story-telling fashion. My family's storytelling style has been added to enhance the listener's (reader's) ability to visualize.

So sit back and visualize as you read the story of Bill Pickett, and remember that everyday people become great heroes as they discover their true purpose. Enjoy!

CHAPTER 1

Billy Is Born

It was about five years after the Civil War had ended, in a place called Taylor, Texas, about twenty-three miles northeast of Austin. On this bright, dew-soaked spring Monday morning, an old black man was sitting on his ragged, wooden porch—worrying, waiting, and rubbing his rough hands together.

Suddenly, the door flew open. A big woman ran out and said, "It's a boy!" The sitting, waiting man was Mr. Pickett, and when he heard the news, he popped up like an exploding firecracker. He hopped around, shouting, "A boy! A boy! It's a boy! My first freeborn son is a boy! Praise the Lord, it is a big, healthy boy!"

He proudly pounced and jumped for joy. He shouted at the top of his lungs until he was wet with sweat and too tired to move. Exhausted, he finally sat down and grinned constantly, showing all thirty-two healthy, pearly-white teeth.

Oh yes, he was proud of that son! Mr. Pickett had been waiting for this son, and he had been planning how he would bring him up to be a God-fearing Christian. He planned to love that little boy always and to be there for him. He often said, "I'll never spoil my son by sparing the rod . . . I'm gonna love him BIG! I will always

make sure that he does the right thing. I will make sure he gets off to a good start. I'm gonna give him two good chores. Yep, I'm a'gonna give him two good chores, and I will always check on him, to make sure that he does them right."

In those days, parents believed that good, hard work made good boys. So his father vowed to train him for two hard, important chores.

CHAPTER 2

Two Simple Jobs

As Billy grew up, his first chore was to doctor all the hurt farm animals. The other chore was to make sure that all the farm animals stayed out of the family garden. Those two simple jobs were learned well by Billy, and they would be a part of his life forever.

Billy's mother taught him to do his first job of doctoring the animals. Billy always paid close attention and asked many questions.

When Billy's mother was showing him

how to fix the broken leg of a chicken, Billy could not stop crying. He could not stop crying because he had seen the mean, huge, huffing, hungry timber wolf bite the chicken and shake him. Billy heard the loud, helpless clucks of the chick, and Billy could feel the chicken's pain.

As he watched his mother doctor the chicken as a teaching tool, Billy memo-

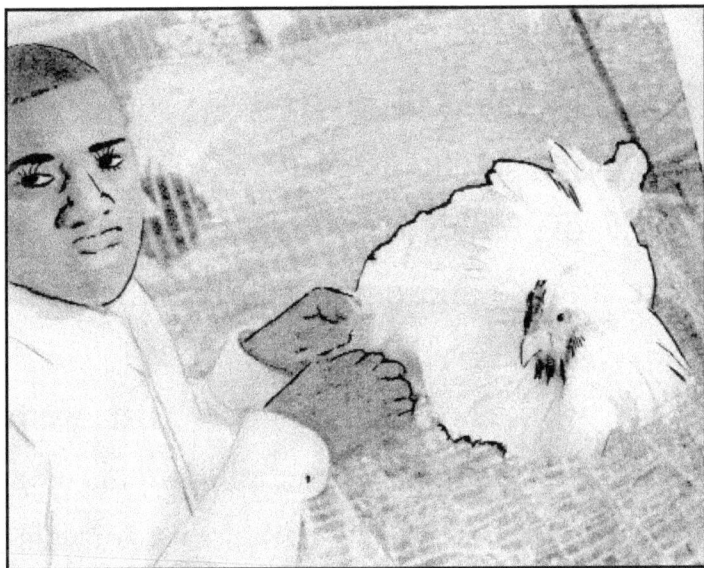

rized every detail of his mother's action. He wanted so very much for the poor chicken to live.

After she thoroughly cleaned the wound, Billy watched his mother pull the leg to straighten the bone. She placed a strong, straight stick beside the bad break in the leg. Then she slowly wrapped smooth, sanitary strips of cloth around the leg and the stick to comfortably bind them together. The chicken cried and struggled. But with a strong, gentle hand, Mrs. Pickett got the job done—and she did it well!

All of Billy's veterinary experiences were intense and emotional like that, but he learned every lesson very well.

He worked on all animals that were brought to him and treated all animals as if they were his own. Billy truly loved animals.

The preacher had said, "Prayer changes things!" Billy really believed that, and so he helped all of his patients get better with hard work and much constant prayer.

Before long, people from all over the county had heard of Billy's great doctoring abilities. One time, a rich man brought his prize goat over 150 miles (from Dallas County) just to let Billy Boy work on him.

Billy fixed that goat's leg. He made him good as new in no time flat.

Doctoring on animals was only one of Billy's chores. He had another one that was important.

Keeping the farm animals out of the family garden was an easy second job, but it required constant attention. The family garden was crucial in those days, because there were no grocery stores like there are today. If the family wanted fresh green vegetables, they had to protect their garden from the animals.

Over a period of time, while doing the same job over and over and over again, Billy got very good at shooing animals away. Yep! That was the case with young Billy Boy. He had been protecting the family garden for so many years that he had accidentally, but thoroughly, developed a style of his own. This style would soon change his whole way of life!

One day Billy was cutting wood on the back porch, as he had done many times before. When he looked up, just like many times before, lo and behold, a cow was in his mother's garden! The cow was chomping on collard greens, as if she had planted and owned the whole garden herself.

Billy could not stand for that to happen. So, he ran and jumped on an unsaddled horse—backwards. Yep ... that is right!

Billy jumped on an unsaddled pony backwards, because that was his highly developed style. He had done this so many times that he did it effortlessly. He grabbed the tail with his left hand and the high mane with his right hand. Billy Boy then gave the horse all of his bare heels, and away they went at full speed, straight in the direction of that outlaw cow.

Boogedy-boogedy-boogedy was the sound they made. Billy and the pony were upon the cow before she could blink an eye or turn her head. Billy had done this so many times that he did not stop, dismount, or even say, *"Shooo, cow, get out of here!"* With a tight leaning bend-over, while on his pony, Billy gave a graceful elbow thump to the cow's ribs. With that thump, he shocked the cow into an immediate jumping run. Breathing hard and with bugged eyes, the cow did not slow down as she leaped the fence like a scolded dog.

Well, Billy Boy didn't think much about this stunt because it was pretty much a daily chore. But someone thought it was amazing. Yep ... someone thought it was truly amazing.

CHAPTER 3

Top-Hand Wages

Not far away, a tall, thin cowboy with a thick blond handlebar mustache was just passing by. His name was Colonel Zack Miller. He saw Billy's amazing feat, and it caused him to smile with joy. He smiled so hard that he burst out laughing. Once laughing, he could not stop until tears came. Then he threw his hat to the ground and said, "Well, bust my britches! That young man is so good at riding bareback that he does it backwards! He can make an outlaw cow behave with the nudge of an elbow. Cows are my business, and I've got to hire that young man. I just got to see if he will work for me." So, Colonel Zack started in Billy's direction as fast as his horse would take him.

Before Colonel Zack could get to that awesome cowhand, he ran upon Billy's father. Colonel Zack immediately said, "Hey, you there ... who is that young man over yonder that handles himself so well?"

Billy's father said, "Aahhhh, that ain't no man. That's Billy Boy, my first freeborn son. He's only fifteen years old."

Colonel Zack said, "Bust my britches again! You mean to tell me that man that handles himself so well is only a fifteen-year-old boy?"

Billy's father stuck his proud chest out, threw his shoulders back, and raised his head and spoke: "Yep, that's what I'm a'telling you."

Now Colonel Zack was even more impressed, so he told Billy's father, "Do you see all that dust that is being kicked up over yonder? Well, that's my cattle drive. Cattle are my business, and I want to hire that son of yours. I'll pay him a dollar a day, and I'll give you thirty dollars right now just to show good faith, and to let you know that I'll look after him as if he were my own son."

Billy's father stuttered, "Y-y-you want to pay him a dollar a day? That is top-hand wages!"

Immediately, Colonel Zack said, "I'm always looking for good men that can handle themselves, and right now I need a good cook."

Billy's father quickly grew sad. He did not want his first freeborn son to leave home at this early age, but he didn't want to stand in the way of a great opportunity. This was a great opportunity! You see, back then, the mayor was the best-paid man in town. The mayor was also the banker. And the mayor only made eighty-five cents a day! So with pride, but sadly, Billy's father yelled out, "Billy, Billy Boy, make haste . . . you come here quick!"

With a fast heel spin, Billy leaped off the porch. He was all stretched out like an attacking wildcat.

He landed on the pony backwards, just as he had done earlier. Quickly, he fastened his right hand to the bottom of the horse's mane. Carefully and slowly his left hand hooked the horse's tail. Then, with the thun-

derous voice of a champion, Billy commanded the horse to make haste to Pappy. Dust flew, and his arrival took place instantly as Billy stopped his horse in front of his father. Billy did a dismount forward roll right off the horse. He landed in front of his father, asking, "Yes, Pap, what do you want?"

Billy's father started chewing him out immediately. "I thought I told you to stop riding so dangerously and to stop showing off so much."

"I ... I ... I wasn't showing off, Pappy, I was just doing it the fun way," said Billy.

Billy's father snapped again, "Well, it don't look fun or safe to me—ANY HOW! I called you over here so that you could make up your mind. Billy, this here is Colonel Zack, and he saw how you were riding that horse bareback with speed ... And he saw how you made that old mean heifer obey with just a good stiff elbow. And he was mighty impressed with you. Billy, he was so impressed that he wants to hire you at top-hand wages—one dollar a day."

Before Billy's father could finish explaining, Billy erupted like a volcano. He leaped almost nine feet straight into the air, tossing his hat straight up until it went out of sight. As he was coming down, he let out a roaring holler of "Yippy-ai-o-kai-yay! How 'bout dat?"

Back on the ground, Billy circled his father with too much energy, as he chanted, "Can I go, can I go, can I go? Daddy, can I go? Pappy, can I go?"

Billy's father was glad to see his son so happy, but he was very sad because he didn't want to see his first freeborn son go off and leave home. Mr. Pickett turned to Zack and said, "Colonel Zack, will you take care of my Billy and look after him as if he were your own boy?"

Colonel Zack said, "I give you my word I will!"

Colonel Zack and Mr. Pickett's eyes were locked for a long minute. Without looking away from each other, both men simultaneously raised their right hands and they spat—wet, loud, and forcefully. They never flinched, and they shook hands strong and long. It was a done deal, and that made it proper.

"Go pack yo' things for the trip tomorrow, Billy Boy. Lord help me . . . I don't know how I'm gonna explain this to your momma. I hope I can get her to understand.

"Colonel Zack, will you stay for supper tonight and leave at first light in the morning? That will make it easier on the boy's momma," said Billy's father.

The Colonel said, "I would be delighted. I thought you would never ask! It has been thirty days since I've had a home-cooked meal, and fifty days since I've slept in a bed."

That night at the supper table, Billy's mother was happy, too, but she could not stop crying. She had prepared a feast that any Thanksgiving Day would be humbled by.

So excited, Billy was eating and talking with his mouth full of food. It was an ugly mess, as food was flying everywhere he

turned his head. Normally, Billy's parents would have corrected him by saying, "Boy, don't talk with a mouth full of food." But they were not thinking straight. They were thinking about losing their son in the morning.

Billy was continually spraying food and talking too much, but it didn't bother Colonel Zack. He held one hand up to shield the food spray, and with the other hand he forked big gulps of food into his large, active mouth.

CHAPTER 4

Yapping and Roping

Colonel Zack really enjoyed the home-cooked feast. He ate three platefuls! After eating, they sat around and listened to Billy talk for almost an hour. Then, with everyone stuffed, they could do nothing but lie down and go to sleep.

All except Billy Boy, that is. Billy was too excited about tomorrow—he could not sleep. The expectations of the new job, the new places and faces he'd see, and the suddenness were just too much for Billy to sleep on. He kept getting up to walk around every fifteen to thirty minutes.

Morning finally came. When the first rooster crowed, Billy had not slept an ounce the whole night. But he sprang from his bed like a fresh rocket. He quickly saddled the Colonel's horse and two others, one for his father and one for himself. Billy knew that his father would ride a mile or two with them to say his fatherly farewells.

Billy went back into the house after washing up. He helped his mother with breakfast. Soon it was time to eat.

Billy was still talking too much. He sprayed everyone with food from his mouth, exactly like he had done the night before. Breakfast came and went quickly, and the three were off.

They were not even one hundred yards

down the road, and the Colonel was wondering if he had made a mistake in hiring Billy because he never stopped talking. As a matter of fact, Billy was getting worse!

Soon they were three miles out, and Billy's father said his final farewell. He told Billy Boy to always obey the Colonel, as if he were his father. Then Pappy turned around and headed back for home.

The Colonel thought that young Billy Boy would quit talking so much now—but he was wrong. Billy turned it up a notch, one more time! Ten miles after Pappy turned back, Billy was still going stronger than ever. The Colonel was starting to wonder if the boy was breathing between sentences. Billy was talking faster than Colonel Zack could think, and it was hurting his head.

The Colonel turned to Billy to tell him to shut up just for one minute, but the innocent look on Billy's face would not allow him to be rude. Still, the Colonel could take no more fast talk, so he kicked his horse and sped up, to ride ahead and get out of hearing range.

Billy did not have the faintest idea why the Colonel rode on ahead, but he kept the same pace, following one hundred yards behind.

After trailing behind for twenty minutes, with no one to talk to, and because he got no sleep the night before, Billy started sleeping in the saddle. He snored so hard that it started to put his horse to sleep. Soon Billy's horse was sleeping and still walking right along. That was a sight to see.

Well, a sleepwalking horse looks funny with his head down to the ground, but it can be very dangerous. Just then, Billy's horse stumbled and almost fell. The near fall quickly woke Billy, and it was just in the nick of time.

The Colonel was still in front, about sixty yards. He was passing by a high peak, and on top of that peak, Billy saw a hungry, huge mountain lion. The mountain lion was crouching down and getting set to leap on Colonel Zack!

Billy had no time for play. Instantly and automatically, he kicked his horse to a full sprint. Then he smoothly grabbed his coiled rope, tossed it, and anchored it in one movement. As the giant cat fell toward Colonel Zack, Billy lassoed that mountain lion right out of midair. This caught Colonel Zack off-guard. But with the same speed and gracefulness that he handled a fork at supper, he drew his pistol and unloaded all six shots right between the killer cat's eyes.

Billy's roping skills left the Colonel with a look of disbelief on his face. Colonel Zack had never seen, known, or even heard of anyone who could rope a cat in midair before. It was so amazing that he said, three times in a row, "You roped that mountain lion right out of midair!" Then, in a flash, the Colonel's mind went back to what he was thinking about before the cat attack.

With fight in his eyes, Colonel Zack yelled at Billy, "Get off your horse, Billy. Get down right now!"

Billy was shocked to hear such a rough and mean sound coming from Colonel Zack. He was even more shocked to see the razor-sharp eyes that were staring at him. With slow, uncertain movement, Billy dismounted and stuttered, "Yes, sir."

Then the Colonel let him have it. He said, "Billy, you were making me sick with all that talk. *Yakety-yakety-yak!* I was just about to pay you off and send you back home because your talk was making my head hurt. Now there—I said it! And then

YOU GO AND SAVE MY LIFE! I just can't figure you out. You almost kill me with your big mouth and all that talk, and then you go and save my life.

"Billy, only two men have ever saved my life before. One died in the Civil War, and the other ... well, there YOU stand! I'm mighty proud that I hired you, because that cat would have made a meal out of me. If you ever need me, you come straight to me! Everyone else has to go to the foreman, but you can come straight to me.

"I praise God that I hired you. You are very handy. But I have one favor to ask of you: between here and Oklahoma, would you please shut your mouth? Don't talk so dad-blame much!"

Billy immediately smiled and said, "Yes, sir, Colonel, I can be quiet as a church mouse. One time I didn't say anything for three whole weeks ..." Quickly, Billy realized that he was doing it again, so he caught himself. He threw his hands up and grabbed his own mouth as if to hold his lips shut.

It took thirty-six days to reach their destination in Oklahoma, but Billy said only four words each day during that time. "Morning, Colonel" and "Night Colonel," and that was plenty enough talk for Colonel Zack. They got along just fine.

CHAPTER 5

Praying for a Friend

After they got to Oklahoma, there was no time for adjustment. Immediately, the foreman showed Billy where he would bunk. He showed Billy the supply wagon, and told Billy the three times daily that they wanted the meals to be prepared. In between meals, Billy would help round up cattle.

Billy went straight to work. Before he knew it, a day turned into a week, a week turned into a month, a month into a year, and suddenly, three years had gone by. The

work was so steady that it all seemed like one big day.

Everyone at the ranch liked Billy Boy. They all took a liking to him from the first day they laid eyes on him. He was the best cook they ever had. Billy did unusual things, like wash his hands before he prepared the meals. Billy also cut off a slice of potato, apple, or pear to test the hot grease. All of the other cooks before Billy had the common habit of spitting in the grease to see if it was hot enough. Another great thing about Billy Boy's cooking was that there was never any cow hair in the food. Yep, everybody loved Billy's proper way of cooking.

Things were going great on every hand for Billy. He saved most of his money, and every month he sent money home to his parents. All of the work hands loved him, and he got along just fine with them.

But something was missing. Something was missing, all right, but Billy could not put his finger on it. Something kept on tugging and pulling at his mind. It was like an empty, alone feeling, even though he was around many people daily and every-thing was going right as rain. No one could look at Billy and tell that Billy's soul was longing for something. He was always so upbeat and positive, no one had a clue.

His lonely feeling grew stronger for about six months, and then one night Billy prayed a different prayer.

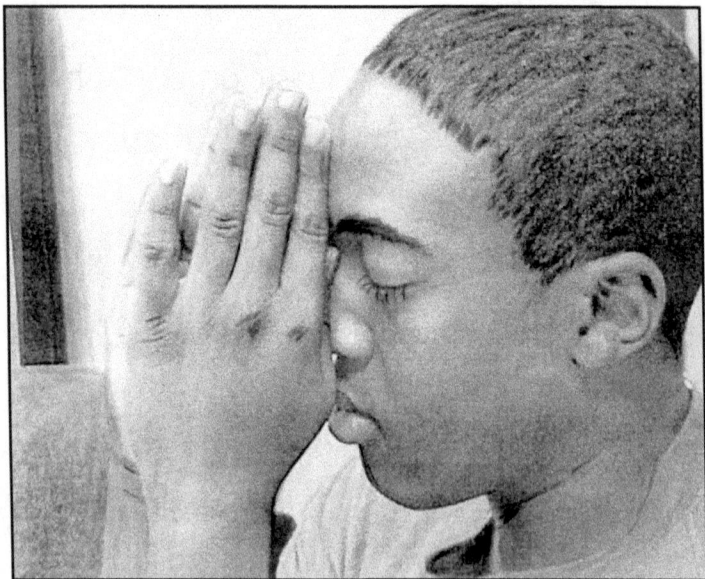

That night, out of desperation, Billy prayed this prayer: "Oh, Lord, thank you for giving me this great job, with so many great opportunities. I am truly thankful for everything. But Lord, I still feel kinda empty and lonely. I feel like I need a special friend. Yes, sometimes I do feel a little funny when the men start telling the old black jokes. But Lord, don't hold that to their account, 'cause You know that they really love me. And you know how they are when they start having fun. Lord, you know that they would fight the devil for me. So that ain't why I feel this way—this is something different.

"Lord, I really don't know just quite how to pray for this, but I reckon I'm asking you to give me a special friend, one that will understand me."

He was about to go on praying, but a loud, demanding voice called out, "Billy! Billy! Billy Boy, come here quick!"

Billy immediately looked up, then jumped up, and said, "Lord, you hear the Colonel calling me ... I'll talk to you later. A-men for now, Lord." Then Billy ran to the Colonel's room and reported, "Yes, Colonel, what do you want?"

The Colonel smiled and said, "Hey, Billy! You know my prize mare is about to foal that colt of hers any day now ..."

Billy was just as excited as the Colonel was. He interrupted the Colonel by saying, "Everybody has been talking about how big she has gotten! They say that baby is going to be a big one. They also say that the baby will be worth three thousand dollars just like its mother, your prize mare!"

Then the Colonel interrupted Billy. "Be quiet a minute, Billy, and listen closely to these here instructions, because the wind is starting to pick up out yonder. Now, back to what I was telling you before you started rambling on . . . I want you to let my prize mare out of her pen. I want her to be able to freely move about when she gets ready to have that baby."

Billy said, "Is that all?" He then clicked his heels like a corporal, saluted like a soldier, and turned and ran to the barn. Billy grabbed the mare by the halter, led her to the door, slapped her on the butt, and let her run free.

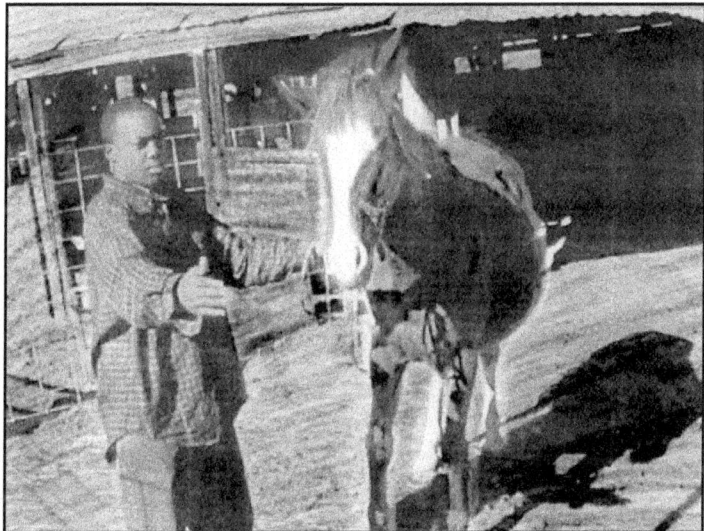

CHAPTER 6

Only Five Hours

When Billy went to bed after letting the mare out, it seemed to be just a normal night.

But later that night, the north wind picked up to almost one hundred miles an hour, and it held steady all night long.

In the morning, at first light, there was a life-changing surprise. Snow had fallen on the ground, as far as the eye could see. It must have been three feet deep. When Colonel Zack looked outside and saw the thick blanket of snow, his bottom jaw practically dropped all the way to the floor and hit like a ton of bricks. For two whole minutes he stood there, in a trance, just looking at what the Lord had done. As he gazed upon the beauty of it, he thought, "The cows will have to dig for food today." Then reality set in. "The cows will dig for food!" Zack shouted as he realized that nothing would be able to eat through that thick barrier of snow. He drew his revolver and fired all six rounds into the air as he shouted, "Men of the 101 Ranch come quick . . . be quick! We have our work cut out for us today. All of

our cows could die, so listen good." He started giving orders and assignments, talking at about one hundred miles an hour. The Colonel was talking so fast that all bystanders could plainly see that old Zack had learned something from Billy Boy.

Colonel Zack was halfway finished when Billy ran into the room. Huffing, puffing, and all out of breath, Billy was yelling at the top of his lungs: "Colonel, Colonel, that prize horse of yours is out there. That mare of yours is in all that snow!" Billy stopped in front of Colonel Zack. He bent over and grabbed his knees, resting and waiting for a response.

The Colonel's eyes bugged out for a second as he realized that truth, but with the focus of a true proven warrior he said, "Billy, this is a cattle ranch. Our money comes from cattle. We don't have time for that old mare now. We've got to feed these cows."

Billy could not believe his ears as he envisioned that horse and her colt, dead and frozen in the snow. The thought caused Billy to yell out, "No, Colonel Zack, I can't leave them out there to die. Colonel, I once saved your life, and I have never asked a favor of you. But it would kill me to do nothing and find them dead later."

The Colonel was cut to the core with Billy's sharp words. Instantly, he replied, "That ain't fair, Billy, for you to use that trump card on me now, at a time like this. A person could die out there! I told your father that I would look after you like my own son." Billy and the Colonel, for the first time ever, were locked in a deep, eyeball-to-eyeball silent staring contest. This went on for a lifetime of seven seconds. Then Colonel Zack said, "I do see the fire of determination in your eyes. I feel your spirit and I can tell that you will never forgive me if I allow you to do nothing. So hear me well, Billy Boy. I will let you go and look, but only because you yelled at me and you pulled the 'I saved your life' trump card for the first and last time. I'll give you five hours to look—but no more. Make sure that you are back and have your chores done! Five hours, Billy. If we have to stop working to come and look for you, I will whip your butt until it ropes like okra."

Billy jumped over and hugged the Colonel and said, "Thank you, Colonel. I'll be safe and I'll make it back." Billy had already saddled his horse before he had stopped to talk with Colonel Zack, and now he was gone in a flash.

CHAPTER 7

The Colt Is Saved—Twice

With speed, Billy looked high but saw nothing. Billy looked low but saw nothing. Three hours had passed and he was starting to feel defeated. At three and a half hours, in desperation, Billy cried out, "Lord God Almighty, maker of heaven and earth, where is that horse? Where would I go if I were that horse in all this snow?" Billy didn't know why he asked like that, but the next words that came out of his own mouth were these: "If I were a horse in all

this snow, I would put my back to Wilson's canyon." With amazement, Billy touched his mouth and repeated what his mouth had just said: "I would put my back to Wilson's canyon?" Billy could not believe the words that had just come out of his mouth. "Thank you, Lord!" he said as he instantly turned his horse in the direction of Wilson's canyon.

Boogedy-boogedy-boogedy! Billy rode his mount at top speed for five minutes, and at nine hundred yards away from Wilson's canyon he saw a speck in the snow. That made him ride even harder. With new speed and thicker snow, the horse stumbled but recovered smoothly. When Billy was only one hundred yards away, he could clearly see the mare, and she had given birth. She had dropped the colt right in the snow.

Billy yelled thanks to the Lord again, and slowed down just enough to lean over and swoop the colt up while passing by. He turned his horse and roped the mother on his way back through. Billy never slowed down to a gallop. He dusted the

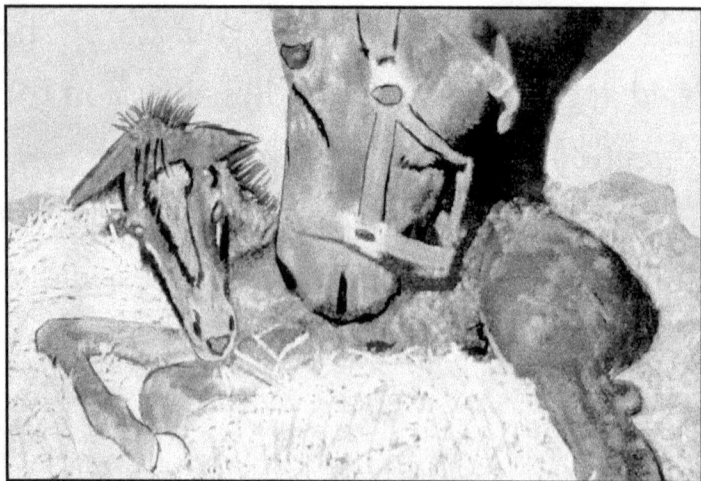

snow off the colt while he rode, holding the colt on his saddle horn.

Gradually, Billy picked up the pace to an all-out run. It was difficult holding the colt and constantly adjusting, while at a full-speed run, but Billy was fluid in the saddle.

Upon arrival at the barn, Billy built a fire to warm the colt. He looked at the clock as he washed his hands to start the supper meal. It had taken four hours and thirty minutes. Billy relaxed mentally because he knew that no one had gone searching for him. He left his horse outside saddled up, as a signal. Riders could see at a distance that he had made it back safely.

Billy started all his chores, then went over to tend to the poor, half-frozen colt. After Billy warmed him up good, he tried to feed him milk, but the weak colt spat it out.

Just then, the Colonel walked in. "Well, Billy Boy, I see you were successful, and that the mare had her colt!" Suddenly, Colonel Zack's eagle examining eyes saw that the colt was shaking like a leaf. He saw that the colt's hair was dried straight, so he was at least six to eight hours old, and he could tell from the deep sink holes in the colt's face that the colt had not had any milk or nourishment in this world since birth.

He drew his pistol slowly and said, "Billy, that colt is dying. We can't let him suffer. We must put him to sleep. Stand back, Billy, and let me put him out of his misery."

Billy leaped to push the gun to the side, and the gun went off. *Boom!*

Colonel Zack was furious as he said, "Billy, you could have killed one of us! Now,

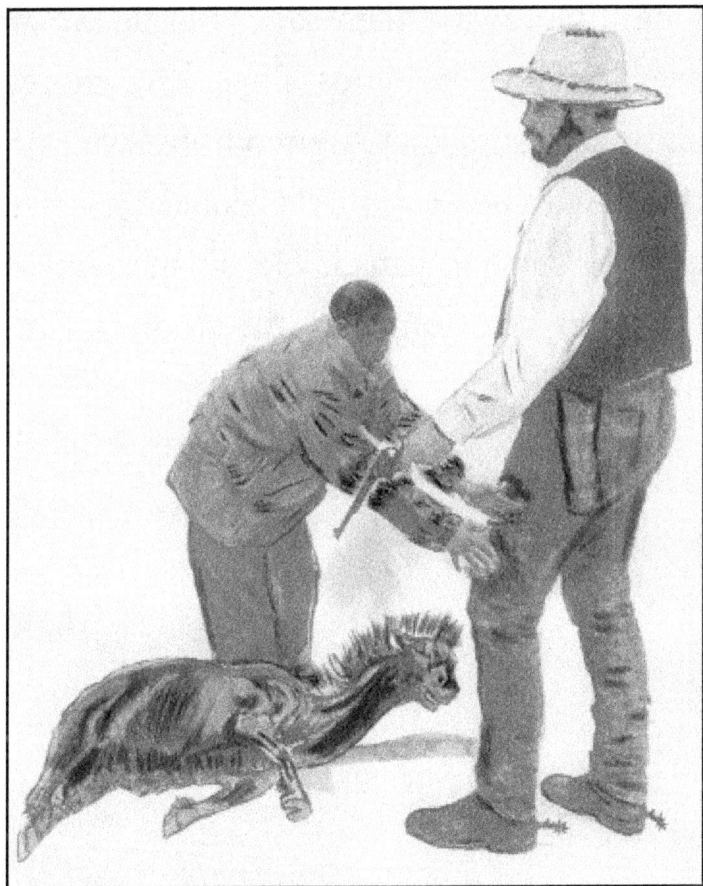

what is wrong with you? You know we are
good people, and that means that we can't
let that colt suffer! I'm sick and tired of
your foolishness!" He glared at Billy for a

long minute, and then said, "Ah, do whatever you want to do! Just finish your chores and make sure that the food is served on time—with no hair in it!" Colonel Zack was red-hot storming mad. He quickly exited the barn and slammed the door behind him.

CHAPTER 8

Answered Prayer

Billy was shaking in his boots, and numb—as if he had been hit in the head with a big stick. Never before had Billy seen the Colonel so mad. With vengeance in his eyes and voice, Billy turned to the colt and said, "Little colt, you are the reason that the Colonel is so mad at me! And now look at you ... you got the nerve to try and die on me! WELL, NO ... YOU ... DON'T!"

Billy grabbed the jug of milk and filled

up his mouth, which made both of Billy's
jaws stick out. Then he grabbed the colt's
bottom lip with his left hand and forced
the colt's mouth open by pulling the top

lip up with his right hand. Billy stuck his lips inside the colt's open mouth and sprayed the milk out. The colt was trying to rebel by spitting the milk out, but Billy knew how to stop that.

He quickly slapped one hand over the colt's mouth as he felt down to the third rib with his other hand. Then he punched the colt right there on that third rib. The result was a loud swallow. *Gump!* Billy repeated the process three more times. As he was about to start the fourth time, the colt let out a loud sound: *Burrrp.* This let Billy know that the colt had had enough. So, every hour on the hour, Billy repeated that process. He was just as faithful as day and night while tending his patient.

Two days came and went, and on the third morning at the five o'clock feeding, he saw that the colt was gone. "Oh, *no!*" Billy panicked as he ran looking here and there. Billy thought the worst, because he knew that before baby animals die they move around looking for a new place.

When he opened the closet door, the colt leaped out and started sucking his face. It looked as if the colt was kissing him right in the mouth! Billy struggled to push the colt back. When Billy won the match, he took the colt to his mother. Immediately, the colt started sucking on his mother. The sucking was so fast, hard, and loud, you could hear it all over the bunkhouse. Billy knew then that the colt would live.

Ecstatic, he ran to find Colonel Zack. Billy found the Colonel with his jaws full of biscuits and syrup. Billy grabbed his hand and said, "Come quickly."

"Must I come now? Can't I finish my breakfast first?"

"No! No!" Billy replied. "Come now!" He practically drug the Colonel, as he led him across the barnyard. When the Colonel saw the nursing colt with his mother, he smiled unexcitedly and said, "Just as I figured," then turned to walk away.

Billy grabbed the Colonel's arm and said, "Don't you know this means the colt will live?"

"Billy, I knew that with your determination that colt had no chance of dying. That's your colt, Billy. I gave up on him, but you did a good job on him. And you kept up with your chores just fine."

Billy backed up and said, "I can't take your prize colt. That is not why I saved him. I just could not stand by and see him die when I knew I could save him."

Colonel Zack drew his pistol and said, "Enough foolish talk! You earned him and you will keep him, or I will shoot him right now."

Billy said, "Put your gun away ... I'll gladly keep him, Colonel Zack." As the Colonel walked out, Billy dropped to his knees and broke out in tears. He was so happy that he literally did not know what to say. Nor did he know what to do. Billy now knew what it was like to be speechless.

He just stayed there, crying and thanking God for this surprise, this gift, this big blessing ... this newfound friend. Then it dawned on Billy that *this* was the special friend he had prayed for a few days earlier. When he realized that God had answered his prayer in this way, his spirit was humbled and he cried out: "Holy is the Lord who has answered me with such an awesome gift. Thank you for this gift, Lord! I receive it, Lord, and I will take good care of it."

His moment of extreme rejoicing was broken when one of the ranch hands named Hank passed by and said, "Are you okay Billy?"

Billy immediately jumped up and said, "Hank, the Colonel just gave me this new colt! I'm going to call him Spradley. Now, after getting a present like this, how do you think I should act?"

Hank said, "Get back on your knees and continue to worship the Lord! If Colonel Zack had gave him to me, I'd thank God for at least a full week!"

CHAPTER 9

A Friend To "Talk" To

That day Billy walked around on a cloud. Everything seemed so bright; everyone seemed so nice; the sun seemed to shine just right; the wind seemed to blow just right. The gift had made it a perfect day.

As Billy went on with his normal chores, he realized that Spradley had spent the whole day with him. Yep, he was right by his side the whole day.

That night Billy dreamed about everything that went on that day. Every place that Billy went, Spradley was there. Every time Billy baked a cake for the men, Billy gave Spradley a bite. Billy still talked too much, but Spradley didn't seem to mind. As a matter of fact, Spradley loved to hear Billy's voice. Yes, this was a match made in heaven.

The next morning came fast. Billy was up at dawn, and this day was just like the day before. Every place that Billy went, Spradley was right by his side. With his newfound friend, Billy talked even more. But Spradley was glad to hear every word. This went on for six months, day in and day out. The time went by so fast because Billy talked all day long.

Before he knew it, another miracle happened. Spradley was able to understand English. Yes, that's right! Billy's big mouth had finally paid off. Spradley could understand every word he said.

With this new miracle, Billy began to use Spradley in his daily job. Billy could often be heard saying, "Spradley, go and get me the butcher knife ... No, not that big one, the one to the right ... Yes, that one." Spradley always got the right one. It was clear that Spradley could understand English perfectly. This might seem unbelievable, but it was true.

Now, back in those days, there was nothing closer to a working man than his horse. Since the beginning of time there had been many famous horse and human friendships. But never before had there ever been and never again will there ever be a horse and man friendship like that of Bill Pickett (the sweat-dirt cowhand) and good old Spradley (the famous cutting horse). They were a match made in heaven; they were best friends.

When Spradley was an eight-month-old, springtime was starting to set in. The melting snow and the long days were waking up all the hibernating animals. One night, a young grizzly bear went down to the 101 Ranch camp. The hungry grizzly was scur-

rying around and looking for food. He had no sooner cut the fence on the chicken house when Spradley's keen ears stood up. Spradley immediately reared up to let Billy know about the danger.

Billy didn't understand. He just looked at Spradley and said, "Settle down and go back to sleep." Spradley was trying to tell Billy something, but Billy was not responding. Spradley had no other choice but to kick the door down with his hind legs. Then he went over to Billy and bit Billy's shirt, holding it tightly between his teeth. Spradley then started to drag Billy out of the front door.

Billy was in shock. Just as he was about to try and figure it out, Billy heard and saw the bear. He realized immediately that Spradley had been trying to talk to him all alone. Billy grabbed the shotgun and shot three times to warn the bear off. That woke up all the men.

Everyone got there just in time to see the bear running away. Billy started jumping and shouting, saying, "Spradley told me that the bear was there! Spradley drug me to the door!" Billy was so excited that Spradley had "talked" to him.

What excitement! What newfound joy! Spradley could talk! These overwhelming thoughts filled Billy's mind. From that day on, Billy started listening as he talked to Spradley. That took their friendship to a new level.

CHAPTER 10

Bulldogging

Three weeks had passed since Spradley first started talking. Billy constantly tried to find ways to spend more time with Spradley. But there are only twenty-four hours in a day, and Billy stayed busy most of the day.

One day he was over at the Miller Outpost Ranch, delivering supplies and feeding the cowhands a lunch meal, when he saw the strangest thing. The Millers had a strange-looking dog from England called a bulldog. That little sixty-five-pound dog could bite an 800-pound cow on the lip and bring him to the ground. Billy thought this was so remarkable, he watched the bulldog over and over again.

As Billy was starting to go back to the 101 Ranch, his mind said to him, "If I could do that bulldog trick, I could save myself two hours a day, and I would have more time to spend with Spradley." Billy thought about that for three weeks, and every day he and Spradley would stop by the Miller Outpost Ranch to look at that old bulldog in action. Billy was afraid to try it, but his desire for more free time drove him to new adventures.

"Four weeks of watching and thinking have gone by ... today is the day," said Billy to Spradley. Billy saddled up his riding horse and rode to the herd.

Billy had gone over this part a thousand times in his head. He picked out the steer that he wanted, and then he chased that steer straight over to the chuck wagon. Billy ran the steer in front of the chuck wagon and jumped off his horse onto the steer's horns. Well, the steer did not like that, and he started to fight. But Billy had his mind made up, and he held on for dear life.

Billy twisted that steer's head forty-five degrees, but the steer would not fall down. Billy continued to twist the steer's head to ninety degrees, but the steer would still not fall down. Billy was getting frantic. He twisted the steer's head to the 180-degree mark! And then he added a little kicking to the steer's knees to help him fall, but the steer stayed up. Billy started to lose hope as he got the steer's head to the 360-degree mark, because the steer was showing no signs of falling.

Billy was just about to give up when he thought how the bulldog made it look so simple. Immediately, Billy's eyes lit up. The bulldog bites his lip! Billy looked at that wet, nasty-looking lip, and he shook his head to say "No way!" But Spradley let out a demanding *"WwHennYES!"* In obedience to Spradley, Billy leaned over and bit the steer on his wet, slobbering lip. Magically, instantly, and miraculously, the steer hit the ground like a ton of loose falling bricks. *Boom-hooffff!*

Billy had wasted forty-five minutes trying to get that steer on the ground, but with this new way of doing things he got the job done with one hour and twenty minutes to spare. He saved so much time with his new method, he decided to do it that way every day.

Anytime you do something every day, you're bound to get good at it. That's what happened to Billy Pickett—he got extremely good at it. Over a two-year period, Billy got so good that he gained two extra free hours each day.

When Spradley was two years old, Billy started riding him. On the day that Billy first rode Spradley, magic took place. Spradley had watched Billy so many times, he knew Billy's every move. Billy's body language, his voice commands—everything fit Billy like a tailored glove. Spradley had been waiting, watching, studying, and anticipating the day that he could carry his best friend. This was remarkable! It was almost as if Spradley could read Billy's mind.

The friendship between Billy and Spradley had become whole. This new combination allowed Billy to do his work with his eyes closed, and it gave him more free time daily. Even when life is great and it seems that all is perfect ... it can get even better.

CHAPTER 11

Do It Again, Billy!

The great teamwork of Billy and Spradley went unnoticed for a long time. Daily they worked on perfecting many team routines that no other man/horse team would dream of. Billy and Spradley were an awesome team; together there was nothing they could not do.

It was inevitable that the duo would be discovered as a once-in-a-lifetime team, but the way they were discovered is very strange.

It happened on an autumn Tuesday in

the high rocky country, when leaves were starting to turn colors for the fall. Colonel Zack had been tracking cougars and wolves for two days when his horse went up a rocky, loose stone trail. The horse slipped and rolled over backwards, breaking Zack's leg in twenty-one places. Zack was brought home in the middle of the morning. He was in plenty of pain as he moaned, groaned, and occasionally yelled bloody murder. He could find relief nowhere as he tossed and turned, holding back the tears.

Suddenly, a loud voice got his attention. It was Billy riding on Spradley. Zack had never seen what was about to happen. Billy rode by, chasing a steer, then jumped off his horse and landed on the steer's horns, immediately bringing the steer to the ground.

Colonel Zack immediately forgot about

his pain and yelled, *"Yi-high!* Do it again, Billy!"

Billy did not know what the Colonel was talking about. Holding on tightly to the steer's horns, Billy said, "Do *what* again? What do you mean?"

Zack shouted with glee: "That steer-busting trick ... do that again!"

Billy did not know how much enjoyment Colonel Zack had gotten out of seeing that. It was like medicine to Zack's aching bones. With blind obedience, Billy did it again, and immediately Zack roared like thunder, "Again Billy! Again!"

Billy did not understand, but he did it seven more times for Colonel Zack. Then he went on and finished his chores, and he thought nothing else about it.

That night after supper, Billy was about

to start on the dishes when Colonel Zack yelled, "Billy, leave those dishes alone and get outside."

Billy quickly replied, "Colonel, I need to clean those plates before the food eats through on them."

"Leave those dishes alone," the Colonel demanded. "Saddle up your horse and show these men your steer-busting trick."

Although he thought this was a waste of daylight, Billy did it anyway because Colonel Zack requested it. Billy saddled his horse and got with it. As soon as Billy hopped on the steer's horns and brought him to the ground, the men went wild, shouting, "*Yi-high!* Come on, Billy, do it again!" Billy was amazed that they liked it so much. He did it seven more times for their enjoyment. Each time, they threw their hats in the air and yelled *"Yi-high!* YOU GO, BILLY!"* Now, in cowboy language that means that they were powerfully impressed.

After showing off, Billy started back inside to wash the dishes. But Colonel Zack stopped him. He said, "Billy, that isn't your job anymore."

"What do you mean?"

"From now on, Billy, we want you to do that steer-busting trick for our show." The 101 Ranch was also home of the 101 Greatest Wild West Show on Earth. From that day on, Billy went all over the world performing that steer-busting trick for kings, queens, noblemen, and anyone who would pay to see the 101 Show. Billy had been discovered!

CHAPTER 12

Not Quite the End

Now you know why and how Bill Pickett became famous and earned his spot in the Legends of the West stamp collection series. But that is not really the end of Billy's story. I'm just pausing here to let some of the readers escape with this fairytale ending. He did live happily ever after. He got married and had children. He saved his money and bought three ranches in his lifetime, one for his brothers, one for his parents, and one for himself.

But there are two more chapters of his life that I reckon I ought to tell. I feel an itch to tell these stories because they are worthy of being heard, and they are powerful lessons and necessary truths about life.

As a good storyteller, I'm giving you a chance to bail out, to stop here and put this book down. Not everyone can take the painful ending that real life often brings.

The following two chapters deal with life struggles. So this is a warning: Do not read the following two chapters until you are ready to deal with the accurate conclusion of Billy's life story.

CHAPTER 13

$5,000 in a Day!

Since you are still reading, you obviously want to know how Billy's life played out. So get yourself comfortable again as this conclusion develops.

Billy had been thoroughly worked by the 101 Ranch for quite a few years, and he was starting to get a little old, gray, and tired. As a matter of fact, Billy was starting to talk about retiring. This talk kept up for about eight months.

When Colonel Zack realized that Billy

was serious, Zack came up with a great idea. He said, "Billy, we've gone through a lot together—thick, thin, snow, sleet, hail, and high water. As a present to you before you retire, how would you like to earn $5,000 in one day?"

"Shucks, Colonel, is it legal?" Billy asked.

"Why, sho' it is. Down there in Mexico City, they have been breeding fighting bulls for years. Now, those bulls down there are much meaner and tougher than the old longhorns that we have up here. Those bulls down there are real killers. We will go down there and make a challenge. We will challenge any one of those matadors to do only half of what you do with one of their bulls. We'll let them know that if any matador can hold on to a fighting bull's horns for five minutes, we will pay him $5,000. Many might try it, Billy, but none will be able to hold on."

Well, they went to Mexico City, and they made the challenge. But after thirty days, not one matador would take the challenge. Not even for $10,000 would one of those matadors get into the arena and try to hold on to a fighting bull's horns for five minutes. All of the matadors were too smart for that. Often when men make dares, good common sense will stop people from taking the dare. That was the case here.

But then something happened. The ladies of the city heard about it, and the beautiful señoritas went to the bullfighting company carrying big signs. They were saying, "Where are all the brave matadors? We can't believe there is not one brave matador in all of Mexico City who can't do what that skinny colored cowboy can do." The bullfighters' union did not know what to do; they had a reputation to live up to.

Fifteen more days went by, but still no one answered the challenge. None of the matadors wanted to die while trying something so foolish. Finally, they could think of nothing else but to reverse the challenge. They offered this challenge to Billy Pickett on a day that the Colonel was not around. Billy thought it sounded like easy money when they said, "Señor Billy, we will pay you $5,000 if you hold on to the fighting bull's horns that we choose." Without thinking, Billy agreed. They spat and shook on it.

Billy was feeling pretty good until Colonel Zack came. When he learned of the deal, he fell to a chair. Grabbing his forehead, he wailed in a loud voice, "Oooohh no, Billy—they reversed it on us. You can't do that, Billy. Let's go and call it off immediately. I'll pay the $5,000. Let's just go and call it off."

"Colonel, I know you said those fighting bulls are awfully tough, but I'm a full-grown man ... and I gave my word. I even spat and shook on it. I must do it. I will do it! My word is my bond."

For the next thirty days, Colonel Zack tried to talk Billy out of it. Billy would not budge.

Finally, the day of the event came. For fifteen miles on either side of the arena, there were horses and buggies tied side by side and row after row after row. Spectators had come in from everywhere. Never before had a crowd like this been seen in one place in Mexico City. Some people had walked over thirty miles and camped out for nights to see this event of a lifetime.

When Billy Pickett rode in on his famous cutting horse, Spradley, the crowd went wild. For five minutes the noise level was so high that two people sitting side by side could not hear each other, even if they yelled in each other's ear. All of the stadium seats were making cracking noises, as if the seats were about to break up from being too full. The stadium was over-packed to the point that if it rained for five minutes straight, no seats would get wet anywhere. Only people would get wet.

As soon as the noise settled down, Billy and Spradley rode in front of the president of Mexico. Spradley took a bow, while Billy tipped his hat. This graceful salute was an act of respect and honor. It made everyone happy, and the crowd went wild again with loud cheering.

No sooner than Spradley had gotten up from his bow, without warning someone opened the gate—and the bull came in.

CHAPTER 14

Little Pepper

This was no small bull. His name, Little Pepper, was a joke. He broke down the half-opened gate that was ten feet tall. His full name was Little Pepper the Widow Maker. He had killed eleven men, and he was looking at Bill and Spradley, sizing them up as victims.

The bull had red, bloody horns from his last fight, and to look at him would bring trembling fear to your backbone. Each time that this monster of a bull drug his

hoof across the dirt, a three-foot-deep trench was left.

After thirty seconds of observing, the bull nodded his head. Then he started his deadly charge. A cold silence fell on the whole arena as Spradley, the experienced cutting horse, froze in place and stood perfectly still. "Hey, move!" someone shouted into the sea of silence.

As the bull drew closer with each thundering stomp, Billy could see that this was a big bull! No, this was a *huge* bull! No, this was a *giant* bull!

The bull approached with lightning speed. The earth was shaking, but Spradley still held his ground, not moving at all. Spradley seemed totally unconcerned about the approaching danger.

As the bull came near striking range, the whole crowd in unison jerked back in their seats, each face with a fretful, fearful look. The spectators anticipated that the bull would finish Spradley and Bill off with no fight.

The bull lowered his head and did not reduce full speed as he carefully pointed his sharp horns toward Spradley's broadside. Now on target, as his horns were about to sink deep into Spradley's side, Spradley leaped straight up into the air with a single motion. To everyone's

amazement, the bull and all danger passed clearly under Bill and Spradley.

Spradley's well-executed move made the crowd go wild again. They said *"Olé!"*

as they threw hats into the arena, two feet deep.

The bull could not stop or turn because of inertia. Quickly, after coming down, Spradley leaped to the bull's side to give Billy his chance. It was only then that everyone understood that Spradley was a master planner and a priceless companion horse. Spradley was bad to the bone!

Now side-by-side with the killer bull because of Spradley's great maneuver, Billy leaped off to grab the bull's horns. Automatic killer instincts caused the bull to fling his head back and toss his horns up to catch Billy in a death trap. Instantly, Spradley realized that Billy, his best friend, was heading straight for death. Spradley stretched to step on the bull's back, which slowed the bull down and broke his focus.

This saving move by Spradley gave Billy time and space to step on the bull's head and remount Spradley in midair. After seeing that, the crowd went *super* wild with cheers! The bull got madder—hateful, head-shaking madder.

After saving Bill, Spradley stopped for an instant by bending his hind legs. This caused the bull to go flying by again, protecting them from hurt. When the bull realized that Spradley had stopped and they were a ways behind, he was burning mad. The bull stopped to turn around, and shook his head from side to side as if in disbelief. The bull stabbed his horns into the dirt. He blew snot and steam from his muddy nostrils. And then he came charging again! No one knew what would happen next—no one except Spradley, that is.

As the bull charged, Spradley sprang to a full charge, going straight in the direction of the bull. Never before had spectators, from anywhere in Mexico, seen or heard of anyone or anything charging a fighting bull like this. *No one charges a fighting bull,* thought everyone. Spectators were grabbing their faces in shock and disbelief.

But Spradley knew what he was doing. The bull was thinking, *I have you in my sights now, and you will not be able to jump over my head this time.* The bull lowered and raised his neck in rhythm as he ran full speed, making sure that if the horse jumped this time he would be ready to jump, too, and catch the horse with his horns. Spradley charged on with the grace and ease of a true champion. He could see the bull's preparation, and he knew that the bull could not anticipate his next move.

Just three strides out before impact, Spradley faked the jump like a good basketball player would do, causing his opponent to go flying into the air uselessly and too early for contact. With all four hoofs firmly on the ground, Spradley made a lateral leap to the right, allowing the airborne bull, Little Pepper, to pass by. Then Spradley made a lateral diagonal leap back to the left, and as he did, he turned around in midair to change direction. This awesome move placed Spradley directly behind the bull, out of sight and pursuing him in a flash.

The bull had lost sight of Spradley for a second because of the high leap, with horns and head tossed straight up. The

crowd roared. No one had ever seen or heard of a horse that could move or even think like Spradley.

Billy jumped to his feet, standing on his saddle while preparing to leap from the invisible position that Spradley had placed him in. But the bull heard Spradley breathing, and Little Pepper turned too fast with pointed horns. Billy barely made it back to the saddle as Spradley leaped to the opposite side, barely escaping death.

Spradley kept putting Billy in great position, but the bull kept answering too fast for Billy to jump on and get a grip. A near miss here and a close miss there—the audience was getting their money's worth! The jostling went on for thirty minutes. The bull was not tiring, but Spradley was slowing. Spradley was wet with thick, white horse sweat.

Billy knew that it would be impossible to grab the bull's horns using Spradley now. He knew that if he were to continue with Spradley, his old friend would get hurt.

CHAPTER 15

Fight to the Finish

Billy rode to the side and said, "I must change horses ... I must change horses!" But the crowd said, "No! No way! The bet will be off if you do that!" Billy shrugged his shoulders and dismounted quickly to lead Spradley out of the arena.

There was no way that Billy would take a chance on getting Spradley hurt. Spradley was his best friend in the whole, wide world.

As they walked out of the arena,

Spradley realized that Billy was quitting. The horse froze in his tracks and shook his head. It was as if Spradley were saying, "No, Billy we don't quit! We came to do a job! The Colonel told you that it would be hard, but you didn't listen! Now get back on my back and let's get this job done! We don't quit!"

Billy tightened up the reins, jerking Spradley and yelling, "Come on! Don't you dare disobey me." He was about to slap Spradley, for the first time ever, to make him leave the arena. But there was no time—the bull was too close.

Billy grabbed the saddle horn tightly, and Spradley took off like a rocket. Billy looked like a waving flag as he pulled himself to the saddle seat. While Billy was pulling himself on, the bull's horn did no damage, but it did hit Billy's foot. Spradley had saved them once again.

The fight was back on, but Spradley knew that Billy would try to quit again. So Spradley went to work. He ran straight into the bull, putting his chest to the bull's rump. Spradley tried to circle the bull constantly to stay out of danger, but the bull jackknifed. His horns sank deep into Spradley's flank. Spradley reared up, showing pain on his face as he whinnied a painful roar ... *"Will-hummbb!"* But Spradley took the pain and held himself in place to give Billy his needed chance. The crowd slumped in agony; they could feel Spradley's pain.

Billy yelled, "Oh, no! Let's get out of here, Spradley!" But Spradley would not move. Billy was crushed, but he could not get Spradley to move away from the killing beast. Spradley painfully waited, insisting that Billy jump on the bull. Billy could see that Spradley still had only one thing on his mind: getting the job done. But getting the job done was not important to Billy now. He yelled, "Spradley, move out or the bull will do you more harm!" Spradley would not move.

The bull was having a field day with Spradley, since Spradley kept backing up so that the bull could not get free. Only seven seconds had gone by, but it seemed like seven years to Billy. He realized that he had to jump on the bull to free Spradley.

"Sss-moo-boooooo" went the bull, as Billy landed on his back, locking himself to the horns. The bull couldn't believe that Billy had done exactly what he wanted him to do. The bull wanted a piece of that man that was sitting on that horse, and now here he was holding on to his horns! Little Pepper leaped for joy. He stood on his hind legs and shook his head to make sure that his kill for the day could not get away. Then he carried Billy to the center of the arena.

Silence once again captured the audience as they saw the bull for what he really was—a calculating man killer.

As soon as the bull reached the center of the arena, he immediately started a head-bucking fit. The crowd expected Billy to be thrown to the dirt. But twenty seconds later, the bull moved from the active cloud of dust. Everyone let out a sigh of relief to see that Billy was still holding on.

This made the bull even madder. He immediately slammed his horns into the dirt and plowed the earth, trying to remove Billy from his head.

After forty seconds of being plowed through the dirt, Billy still held his ground. Now with blood-red angry eyes, the bull raised his hind leg and tried to scratch Billy off like a hound dog reaching for ticks behind the ear. The hoof was bruising Billy's back. Billy adjusted, and the bull started kicking his own back.

Billy was winning, and the crowd cheered him on. Who would have thought that a man could hold on to a 3,000-pound fighting bull's horns for over two minutes without being killed? The audience increased their cheering, which made the bull go wild. Little Pepper was now drunk with frustration. Billy was right there on his head, but the bull could not get to him. Acting as if he could take it no longer, Little Pepper rolled over and over in the dirt, banging his head on the earth. But Billy still held on.

Finally, the bull stopped, stood up, and then stood perfectly still for ten seconds. He looked as if he were frozen, and that sent chill bumps all over every spectator. Everyone knew that a fighting bull never quits; he fights until he dies.

Little Pepper the Widow Maker's eyes grew red, redder, reddest. Then he let out a bellow of victory: *"Ka-booooo!"* The bull looked at the far wall and pinpointed a spot on it. The crowd cried in unison, "Oh, no!" as the bull picked up full speed and ran into the wall, head first. *Booom!* The bull broke five of Billy's ribs. The crash also left the bull unconscious.

Billy thought this was the end; he thought the bull was dead. But as he was about to let go, the bull leaped to his feet again, shaking his head and bucking like a bronco. He looked around for Billy, to finish him off, and realized that Billy was still hanging on to his horns like a rag doll! This made the bull spitting mad. He bellowed at Billy now constantly, *"Sha-mooo, Sha-mooo!"* The bull wanted a clear shot at Billy. He was not going to quit.

As Little Pepper started to repeat his efforts to get Billy off, Colonel Zack jumped up and shouted, "It's been five minutes—get him out of there!" But no one responded to help. The Colonel saw that they all knew the time was up, but they wanted to see more action. He jumped up and shouted again, this time firing his pistol into the air. "It's been five minutes—get him out of there!" Still, no response.

Colonel Zack then shouted, "Men of the 101 Ranch, get down there with your ropes and get Billy out of there. We will cover you." They had to get fifty-seven ropes on that bull to bring him down, and it was just in time. Little Pepper was trying to do that suicide run into the wall again at full speed. Surely that would have finished off old Billy.

CHAPTER 16

Let Him Live

With busted ribs, and looking like a mud-ball, Billy limped over to Spradley. Leaning against the arena wall, Spradley was shaking like a thin leaf in the wind. He had lost a lot of blood and was getting ready to drop.

When Billy saw Spradley close up, he burst into tears. "Oooh, what have I done for money? Have I killed my best friend?" Then, out of nowhere, that fighting cowboy spirit kicked into Billy. He threw his shoulders back as if he had no busted ribs. And the look on his face said, "Death, I'll fight you, and I'll fight you good for Spradley!"

Billy shouted, "I'll pay any man anything if he can save Spradley."

One of the Hispanic cowboys from the 101 Ranch said in Spanish, "Someone go and get me some red bananas." Thirty seconds later, a man from the crowd came back with green bananas. "No, no, no, I said *red* bananas." Thirty seconds after that, someone arrived with red bananas. The cowboy peeled the bananas and pushed them into the bull horn holes that were still bleeding on Spradley's flank. This finally stopped the bleeding, but Spradley was too weak to walk.

They built a stretcher to get the horse out of the arena. A truck was used to get him to the train, and the train got them back to Oklahoma.

Well, the long ride was not good for Spradley. Infections set in, and then fever. Spradley got pneumonia, and then he was too weak to eat. One bad thing after another kept happening, for one month, then two, then three months. It was in that sixth month that everyone told Billy it was hopeless. But Billy gritted his teeth and prayed even harder.

"Lord, all of this was my fault. I was just greedy for more money, and now Spradley is suffering. Please, Lord, don't take his life. Please let him live." The prayer reminded him of the good feeling he got when he prayed over hurt animals as a boy.

That night Billy fell asleep on Spradley's

chest. He slept peacefully for the first time since the night before the action in Mexico City. That night Billy dreamed that Spradley had died.

The next morning, a crowing rooster woke Billy up. Spradley was standing over him, and this was not a dream! Billy leaped up and hugged Spradley around the neck. Spradley had finally stood up, and from that day Spradley moved to great recovery.

Recovery does not always mean that everything goes back to normal. Billy could never do those dangerous tricks with Spradley again, nor could he do simple things like roping. But Billy didn't mind. He had his best friend with him, and Billy was so, so happy.

CHAPTER 17

The Colonel's Eulogy

Not many people can boast daily about the good life they have lived, but Billy's constant enjoyment allowed him to rejoice and boast every time he opened his mouth. He had a grateful spirit after retiring. Although arthritis rode him hard every day, because during his life he had broken almost every bone in his body, Billy always had a pleasant word for everyone. Not only did he have a good word for everyone that he met; he always had plenty of exciting stories to tell. Everyone loved to be around Billy. Every story would keep listeners sitting on the edge of their seats, with eyes bugged and mouths open.

Bill Pickett was one of the last hard-nose, stalwart cowboys who helped to tame the West. At the age of sixty-two, retired living was so good that it made Billy twenty pounds overweight. But 165 pounds still looked good on him. Biting steers had made him toothless, but he could still chew a side of beef like a hard-working, twenty-year-old top hand.

Even though he had bought three ranches, he still preferred to live at the 101 ranches with lifelong friends. Life was going great at the 101. Then times started changing, and a little trouble set in.

As more and more people moved in and

settled out west, the land changed. Population and lifestyle started to be the problem. Cars were replacing horses; machines were replacing men; people were starting to live much closer together; few people farmed or even had gardens; and the world did not look the same. The world had its first world war, then the country went into a depression.

The 101 Ranch was not affected by all the changes—until the depression hit in 1929. That depression caused the 101 Ranch to no longer be sheltered. It was in 1931 that the depression closed the 101 Wild West Show.

"With changes all around you, no one ever knows what day will be your last. So, enjoy every day to the fullest," Billy would say. "Remember to say thank you to people you are thankful for. Say you're sorry right there when you step on someone's toes. If you say you're going to do something, then do it. Never put off for tomorrow what you can do today." All of these phrases were Billy's popular sayings, and some of his final words.

It was April 2, 1932, on a fresh spring morning, when good-humored Billy was passing by the wild horse corral. He spotted the fresh new herd that had just been captured. It wasn't the herd that got Billy's attention, but a young, three-year-old stallion. This stallion was remarkable, because he looked exactly like old Spradley! Billy could not believe it. Even though he knew it wasn't Spradley, he just had to get a closer look. Billy's idea of a closer look was to cut him out of the herd and get a saddle on him.

But what happened was not in the plan. The worst thing that you could imagine happened.

People can be like horses and horses can be like people in many ways. There are people all over this world who have look-alikes. But when you talk to their look-alike, or see the way they act or hear the way they think or observe things they do, you quickly realize they are totally different from their look-alike. In some cases they are total opposites of their look-alikes. Look-alike horses are the same as look-alike people, and that is what Billy discovered that day.

The horse that looked exactly like Spradley did not act like Spradley at all. As soon as Billy roped him, the wild horse reared up. He was pawing with his front

hooves as he ran toward Billy. Billy didn't have enough time to get out of the wild horse's way. He didn't have a chance to deal with this surprise.

The wild horse pawed him to death. It was hard to believe. Billy was killed by a Spradley look-alike.

Colonel Zack made it back late that evening. When he found out what had happened, he fell to his knees right there in the dirt, as if someone had ambushed him and shot him right through the heart with an arrow. Then he cried loudly like a baby, with no comfort. The Colonel stayed there on the ground for hours, just sobbing.

When he got up, he wiped his face with dirty hands. Then he went to the corral and shot that wild horse right between the eyes.

Billy's funeral was two days later. More than 2,000 people attended.

Colonel Zack was still a man of few words. But he was so moved with the life of Billy, he wrote these words and spoke them at the funeral: "Billy, I'm going to miss you. You're the whitest black man that I've ever known." And then he started to read this:

"Old Billy has died and gone away, over the great Divide, gone to a place where the preachers say, both saint and sinner will abide.

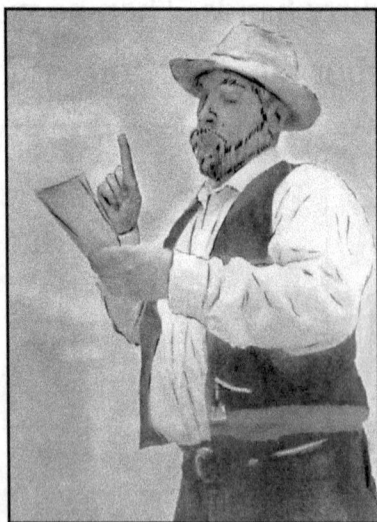

If they check his brand like I think they

will, it's a running hoss that they will give to Bill. And some good wild steers till he gets his fill, with a great big crowd for him to thrill.

"Billy's hide was black but his heart was white; he'd sit up through the coldest night, to help a dogie in a dying fight, to save a dollar for his boss. And all Billy wanted was a good fast hoss. Three square meals and a place to lay, his tired self at the end of the day. If the job was tough, be it hot or cold, you could get it done if Billy were told. He'd fix the fence or skin a cow, or ride a bronc or even plow, or do anything if you told him how. Like many men in the old-time West, on any job he did his best.

"He left a blank that's hard to fill, for there will never be another Bill. Both white and black will mourn the day that the Biggest Boss took Bill away."

Colonel Zack sat down and did not speak another word for a whole month.

Bill Pickett did not set out to become one of the most famous legendary heroes of the West when he left home—but it happened. I think it was because he kept a pure heart, he always did the best that he could do, and he called upon God for help. Now, that is a lesson for me and you.

We are all legends in our own times, waiting to happen!

Texas State Historical Marker honoring Bill Pickett.

The great Bill Pickett lived a full and purposeful life. In 1890 he married Maggie Turner, and they were the parents of two boys and seven girls. The inventor of "bulldogging" was inducted into the National Cowboy Hall of Fame in 1971, long after his death. But this was a major accomplishment, since he was the first African American inductee.

Bill lived in a time when segregation was rampant in the United States. Most public places, such as restaurants, allowed only white people to enter. African Americans were even forbidden to use public restroom facilities and drinking fountains, unless they used those labeled for "colored" people only.

The 101 Ranch was one of the few places where a man was paid for his work, and skin color made little difference. He was always treated with great respect by Colonel Zack Miller.

Some of the quotes from Colonel Zack at Bill's funeral sound horribly racist today ("the whitest black man I've ever known" and "Billy's hide was black but his heart was white"). But his statements were meant only as the highest praise. Colonel Zack was present at the burial of many friends, but he was never emotionally moved to write a eulogy until his friend Billy died. Although his words reflect the terrible injustice of those days, he was showing the deepest respect that he could muster for a friend. Isn't that a lesson in sociology, and the changing of the times?

GLOSSARY

accurate: exactly correct.

ambushed: attacked from a hidden position.

arthritis: an inflammation of the joints which causes pain.

bellow: to roar deeply, as a bull does.

body language: communication through body movements and facial expressions.

broadside: to strike at full speed on the side.

bronco: a wild horse that hasn't been broken for saddle riding.

bulldogging: throwing down a calf or steer by grabbing the horns and twisting the neck.

bunkhouse: sleeping quarters on a ranch.

chuck wagon: a wagon equipped with food and cooking supplies, used on a ranch.

collard greens: leaves of kale, a vegetable.

cutting horse: a horse used by cowboys to round up cattle.

dogie: stray or motherless calf.

ecstatic: overjoyed.

feat: a notable act of skill.

flank (noun form): the side of a person or animal, between the last rib and the hip.

flinched: jumped or moved from surprise or pain.

fluid (adjective form): smooth and flowing; graceful.

foal: the offspring of a horse.

foreman: one who leads a work crew.

freeborn: born as a free person, not as a slave.

halter: a rope or leather strap used to lead or secure an animal by the head.

heifer: a young cow, particularly one that hasn't given birth.

hyperbole: exaggeration used for emphasis or effect.

inertia: resistance to movement or action.

inevitable: impossible to avoid.

jackknifed: folded or bent like a clasp knife that folds up.

keen: sharply sensitive; strong.

lassoed: captured with a noosed rope.

lateral: at or to the side.

maneuver: a controlled movement.

mare: female horse.

matador: bullfighter.

mount (noun form): a horse that is being ridden.

obedience: properly carrying out orders or instruction.

Ole!: (Spanish) a cheer of approval.

reared up: stood up on the hind legs.

saddle horn: the knobby part of a saddle, used for tying rope to.

spectators: those watching an event.

stalwart: possessing great strength.

steer (noun form): a young male bovine animal.

trump card: a card held in reserve for winning a trick in a card game.

unison: at the same time.

veterinary: relating to animal medicine or health.

BIBLIOGRAPHY

Anderson, LaVere. *Saddles and Sabers: Black Men in the Old West*. Champaign, Illinois: Garrard Publishing Company, 1975.

Durham, Philip C., and Everett L. Jones. *The Negro Cowboys*. Lincoln, Nebraska: University of Nebraska Press, 1965.

Hanes, Colonel Bailey C. *Bill Pickett, Bulldogger: The Biography of a Black Cowboy*. Norman, Oklahoma: University of Oklahoma Press, 1977.

Johnson, Cecil. *Guts: Legendary Black Rodeo Cowboy Bill Pickett: A Biography*. Fort Worth, Texas: The Summit Group, 1994.

Katz, William Loren. *The Black West*. Seattle, Washington: Open Hand Publishing, Inc., 1987.

O'Brien, Esse Forester. *The First Bulldogger*. San Antonio, Texas: The Naylor Company, 1961.

Pinkney, Andrea Davis. *Bill Pickett: Rodeo Ridin' Cowboy*. New York, New York: Harcourt Brace & Company, 1996.

ABOUT THE AUTHOR

MALCOLM DICKINSON was born in Aliceville, Alabama, in 1953. With parents in the military, his mobile childhood took him from New Mexico to Georgia, Germany, and Fort Hood (Texas). Most summers were spent on his grandfather's farm in Aliceville.

After graduating from Killeen High School, Dickinson attended Prairie View A&M University on a full track scholarship. He obtained a master of education degree in English and administration from Prairie View and Tarleton State University. Upon graduation from college he was commissioned into the

U.S. Army as a Signal Corps second lieutenant. He served five years in the military.

Dickinson's teaching career began in Wagner/Salley, South Carolina, and he subsequently taught English and coached soccer for nine years at Killeen High School in Killeen, Texas. Currently he is associate principal at Copperas Cove (Texas) High School, where he has worked for ten years.

Malcolm Dickinson is a fisherman, horseman, hunter, and one of the last trackers. He continues his family's storytelling tradition as an educator and participates in various storytelling events. He has been married to Patricia Ann (Sewell) Dickinson, an educator, for twenty-seven years, and they have four sons.

www.ingramcontent.com/pod-product-compliance
Lightning Source LLC
Chambersburg PA
CBHW060016050426
42448CB00012B/2782